FOR
CHILDREN
ONLY

VOLUME II

A BOOK OF OBJECT
LESSONS
FOR YOUNG CHILDREN

Order this book online at www.trafford.com
or email orders@trafford.com

Most Trafford titles are also available at major online book retailers.

Note for Librarians : A cataloguing record for this book is available from Library
and Archives Canada at www.collectionscanada.ca/amicus/index-e.html

Printed in Victoria, BC, Canada.

ISBN : 978-1-4269-1622 9 (sc)

*Our mission is to efficiently provide the world's finest, most comprehensive book publishing
service, enabling every author to experience success. To find out how to publish your
book, your way, and have it available worldwide, visit us online at www.trafford.com*

Trafford rev. 9/10/2009

 www.trafford.com

North America & international
toll-free : 1 888 232 4444 (USA & Canada)
phone : 250 383 6864 ♦ fax : 812 355 4082

Dedication

To our sons, Kevin and Troy
Our daughters-in-law, Beth and Erika
Our five grandsons, Pierce, Joe, Luke, Andrew and Jacob
And especially, my husband, Lowell, who has lived his life before
his family
As a sermon well preached.

Preface

These object lessons are especially for young children, preschool or early elementary school. They are meant for interaction with the children. Allow the children to be a part of the discussion. If you are using these stories as children's sermons, get on their level visually. Talk to the children, not to the congregation. This is your time with the children. If something triggers their memory to this thought years from now, you want them to remember that they were loved and listened to.

The same goes for parents using these for their own devotional time with the young children. Make this their time. Let these open up a discussion that may lead to other topics of discussion.

Use these as they are or alter them to suit your situation but enjoy the time with the children. You will be blessed and so will they.

Contents

Contents

Listed by books of the Bible

1
Benediction

Thought : The best that we can wish for another is "God's peace."

SCRIPTURE : "And the peace of God, which transcends all understanding, will guard your hearts and minds in Christ Jesus." Philippians 4 : 7 NIV

LESSON : {Read the scriptures.] [Say.] We often hear this scripture used as a benediction or a blessing at the end of a worship service. Maybe you have heard your pastor or someone say this verse. The peace of God is the greatest wish we can bestow on another. This scripture says that it will "guard" our hearts and minds.

When we become upset, anxious, or troubled, God's peace can calm our anxious hearts. It keeps us from "falling apart." It also protects us from evil. Let us thank him for that peace.

PRAYER : Thank you Dear God for the peace that you bring to our lives, for the fact that we can trust completely in you. Amen.

2
A Checker Game

OBJECTS : Checkerboard and checkers.

SCRIPTURE : " Let us not give up meeting together" Hebrews 10 : 25 NIV

LESSON : (Ask) Who has played checkers? You know that the object of the game is to jump; to capture the other person's checkers.

(Show the board with the checkers set up. On one side have the checkers close together. On the other side leave a few "alone".)

(Say) In checkers it is important to keep your checkers together so that they do not get caught.

This game reminds me of church attendance. As we stick together in church we are stronger. It is easier to live for God when we come together for worship.

We need to come to church. The Bible tells us not to forget to assemble ourselves which means to come together for worship.

PRAYER : Thank you Lord for the joy we get as we worship. Amen.

3
A Cheer For Jesus

OBJECT : A pompom or a school pennant.

SCRIPTURE : " O, praise the Lord, all ye nations; praise him all ye people. For his merciful kindness is great toward us; and the truth of the Lord endureth forever. Praise ye the Lord."   Psalm 1 : 7 KJV

LESSON : (Show the pennant or pompom) (Ask) How many of you like to go to a ball game? Do you like to cheer and yell for your team? Do you say good things about the team and praise them? We can have a good time at the ball game.

The Bible teaches us something else about praise. (Read the scripture.) We are to offer praise to God. We are to be happy and joyful when we come into God's house. We have much to thank him for. Let's remember to be happy and praise God.

PRAYER : Thank you God for creating us; for giving us a reason to be happy. In Jesus name, Amen.

4
A Cold Drink

OBJECT : A cup of cold water.

SCRIPTURE : "And whosoever gives to one of these little ones even a cup of cold water to drink, truly I say to you he shall not lose his reward." Matthew : 10 : 42 KJV

LESSON : (Show the glass of water with ice cubes in it). (Read the scripture.) (Ask). When you are thirsty, what is the best thing you can drink? Water. Water will stop our thirst more than any other drink. Just imagine being hot and drinking a big glass of water. Doesn't the water taste good? The Bible tells us to do good deeds for others. Do things that help others fell better. Even little things encourage others. We are to do our good deed in the name of Jesus.

PRAYER : O Lord, help us to remember to do good deeds for others to show that we love you and to show that we love others. Amen.

5
A Gift

OBJECT : Tiny wrapped gifts for each child : gum, candy, tiny toy, etc.

SCRIPTURE : "Behold, children are a gift of the Lord." Psalm 127 : 3NAS

LESSON : [Ask the children if they like gifts.] [Let them share their thoughts.] [Say.] Gifts are special. The one who gives the gift is also special.

[Read the scripture.]

[Ask,] Who is the gift? Yes. Children are the gift.

[Ask.] Who is the giver? The Lord. The verse says that children are a gift from the Lord. That means that you were a gift. That must make you feel pretty special. You are a gift from the Lord to your families. You are special and the Lord is special because he is the giver of all gifts.

PRAYER : Thank you Lord for children; for *these* children and the joy that they bring to others. Amen.

6
A Good Helper

OBJECT : A pair of dark glasses; a magnifying glass.

SCRIPTURE : " (The Lord came) to open blind eyes." Isaiah : 42 : 7 NAS

LESSON : Show the pair of dark glasses and/or the magnifying glass. (Ask) Do any of you have a friend or a relative that is blind? Let them share. (Read the scripture) (Say) Sometimes a blind person is made well either through surgery or through other ways. God may help them to see. Sometimes they remain blind. There was a blind elderly lady who had a young friend like you. He went to see her daily; he would read to her, help her with chores, and walk with her. In a way, he helped to "open her eyes". You could be a helper to someone blind or to one who has very bad vision.

PRAYER : Our Father, thank you for showing us ways we can help others. In Jesus name. Amen

7
A Lighted World

OBJECT : A lighted globe or a globe with a spotlight on it.

SCRIPTURE : "You are the light of the world." Matthew 5 : 14 NAS

LESSON : (Show the globe.) (Help the children locate the place where you are living.) (Talk about how the light helps you to see the "world" on the globe.)

(Read the scripture.) (Say.) The Bible tells us that (you) all of us are the light of the world. Just as the light inside the globe helps us to see, we are the "light" that helps others to know about Jesus. We can help others to follow the right way. We are a light for Jesus in this world.

PRAYER : Thank you our Father for letting us be a light for others. We know that this is possible only as you help us.   Amen.

8
A Noisy Gong

OBJECTS : A pair of cymbals or something similar to hit together. If possible, give each child some type of noisemaker.

SCRIPTURE : "If I speak with the tongues of men and of angels but do not have love, I have become a noisy gong or a clanging cymbal." 1 Cor. 13 : 1 NASB

LESSON : [Show the cymbal; hit it together to make a loud sound. Let the children use their noisemakers to make a sound.]

[Read the scripture.]

Now have the children whisper with you; "I love you."

[Ask] Which is the more pleasant sound?" The 'I love you' or the 'loud noise'? We are told in the Bible that our love is to be real, not just a lot of noise. We can show that our love is real by the way that we treat other people. If we are caring and kind, our love will not be just words or noise; it will be real.

PRAYER : Thank you for the love, O Lord that you give to us. Thank you for a love that helps other people. In Jesus name. Amen.

9
A Witness

OBJECT : A "pretend" subpoena.

SCRIPTURE : " You will bear witness also, because you have been with me from the beginning." John 15 : 27 NAS

LESSON : (Show the piece of paper.) (Say) When a person has seen a crime, an accident, or knows something to be true they are often given a "subpoena" to appear in court. They are asked to tell what they saw and/ or heard. Because they were present, they are a witness. A witness is one who sees or knows that something took place.

(Read the scripture). (Say) Jesus disciples had been with him daily. They know all about him. Now they were to tell others what they had seen and heard.

Today we continue to be witnesses as we share the good things we know about Jesus.

PRAYER : Father, help us to be a true witness of your love and power. We pray in Jesus name. Amen

10
Abide In Jesus Love

OBJECT : a piece of' green' clay or play dough and a piece of clay that has hardened into shape.

SCRIPTURE : "Just as the Father has loved me, I have also loved you; abide in my love." John 15 : 9 NAS

LESSON : Show the clay that is soft and workable. Show the hardened clay. [Read the scripture.] "Just as the Father has loved me, I have loved you; abide in my love."

[Say.] Jesus told his followers to abide in his love, to stay in his love, to live in his love. As long as we stay in his love we are like the workable piece of clay. He can help us to grow, to continue to change and become better people. As long as someone is working with the clay it can be changed; once it is left alone, it hardens and cannot be used. We must not stay away from Jesus' love or his people. Let us stay near to Jesus and strive to become like him.

PRAYER : Our Father help us to stay close to you and to your people. Help us to become more like Jesus. Amen.

11
Access To Gods's House

OBJECTS : A picture of a castle with a moat around it or a picture of any type of building that it is very difficult to visit.

SCRIPTURE : "I was glad when they said unto me, "Let us go to the house of the Lord." Psalm 122 : 1 NASB

LESSON : [Pass the picture around.] Let the children tell you what it is. [Ask]. Have you ever been to a castle? Have you ever seen a beautiful building or some very interesting building that you could not enter? There are places that we would like to see, but because of security to the nation or for other reasons we are not allowed to enter.

I want you to think of a building where you are always welcome. Did you ever think how easy the church is to get into? Just look at the number of doors coming into the sanctuary. Think how many doors open to the outside. Perhaps there was an usher greeting you at the door as you came in today. Isn't it wonderful to have a place where you are always welcome? Aren't you glad our church doesn't have a moat around it, or bars on the door, or guards at the door to allow only a select few inside? God welcomes us all into his house to pray and to worship him. Let us thank him.

PRAYER : Thank you dear God for our church, for the freedom to come here, and for the warm welcome we find here.   In Jesus name we pray. Amen.

12
Balm For Pain

OBJECT : A jar of healing ointment or soothing lotion

SCRIPTURE : "Suddenly Babylon has fallen and been broken; wail over her! Bring balm for her pain; perhaps she may be healed." Jeremiah 51 : 8 NASB

LESSON : {Show the ointment.] [Say.] When you get hurt, Mother may say, "Let me put this on your cut; it will make it feel better."

It soothes the hurt. [Read the scripture.] This verse makes reference to a "broken" country. The word "balm" means healing. Not only do individuals need healing, sometimes nations need healing and restoring to the power of God. Only He can bring that power or that balm. Let us pray that He would be at work in our own country; that we will feel the balm of his healing power.

PRAYER : Thank you O Lord for our country. Thank you for our freedom. Help us to stand out as a nation whose trust is in God.

In Jesus name. Amen.

13
Behind Masks

OBJECT : paper masks for each child.

SCRIPTURE : "Keeping a close watch on Him {Jesus} they [the scribes and chief priests] sent spies who pretended to be honest. They hoped to catch Jesus in something he said so that they might hand him over to the power and authority of the governor." NIV

LESSON : {Read the scripture.} [Say] We read many times in the Bible about people who pretended to be someone that they were not. Usually we associate this pretense with bad. Jesus sees us as we really are so why should we pretend to be something else. [Show the mask.] Have you ever played a game and pretended to be someone else? A game is fun; however in real life let us remember who we really are. We belong to Jesus. He knows who we are.

PRAYER : Thank you Dear God for loving us just as we are. Amen.

14
Being On Time

THOUGHT : "A diller, a dollar, a ten o'clock scholar; what makes you come so soon? You used to come at ten o'clock and now you come at noon." Mother Goose

SCRIPTURE : "It is time to seek the Lord until He comes to reign righteousness on you."   Hosea 10 : 12 b NASB

LESSON : Repeat the nursery rhyme. (Ask) How many of you have heard this rhyme before? In reality the nursery rhyme may not make a lot of sense. It means that the once prompt schoolboy is now late. Teachers don't like that. Just as we are to be prompt at school and work, we should be on time for Sunday school and worship. The scripture says, "It is time to seek the Lord.....". Let's be eager to come to His house. Come to Sunday school with a smile; come to worship with a "happy face". Show that you like to be in God's house. Let's not be like the late scholar. Let's be on time.

PRAYER : Thank you Lord, for these boys and girls. Help them to be glad to come to your House. Amen.

15
Binding Up Wounds

OBJECTS : Gauze, tape, band aids.

SCRIPTURE : " Praise the Lord, for it is good to sing praise to our God; He heals the broken hearted and binds up their wounds."   Psalm 147 : la NASB

LESSON : (Show the objects used in treating wounds). (Ask the children to remember a time when they fell or hurt themselves). (Say) Do you remember how the bandage made your injury feel better? Do you remember the special attention you received then from your family? (You may let one of the children share an experience).

(Read the scripture).   The Psalmist rejoiced and praised God because God had helped him. Perhaps God did not actually tie up an injury but he had helped him. The scripture mentions that "he binds up the broken hearted". Brokenhearted are those who are upset, troubled, and cannot help themselves. That is when Jesus helps us. He does what we cannot do.

PRAYER : Thank you dear Jesus for 'binding up' our hurt feelings, our sadness and our worries. May we always be thankful to you. We pray in Jesus name. Amen.

16
Bound Together By God

OBJECT : a spiral notebook with a different word or picture on each page.

SCRIPTURE : "For you are all sons of God through faith in Christ Jesus. " Galatians 3 : 26 NASB

LESSON : {Show the notebook.} [Say.] Each page of this book is different from the other pages. It has a different word, or pictures. It is still a part of the book. It is bound to the book by the spiral that holds it together. Let us think about the church membership. We are all different. We represent different occupations. Some are farmers, fisherman, businessmen, teachers, etc. There are all kinds of people, however one thing binds us together. That is our faith in the Lord Jesus.

[Read the scripture.] "For you are all sons of God through faith in Christ Jesus."

So this is what a church is- a group of people bound together by their faith in Jesus.

PRAYER : Thank you Jesus that you bind us together with your love. Amen

17
Built To Stand

OBJECT : Brick, cement, nails, hammer or building materials.

SCRIPTURE : " In whom the whole building, being fitted together is growing into a holy temple in the Lord." Ephesians 2 : 21 NASB

LESSON : [Show the building objects.] (Ask.) What is our church made from? (Allow the children to respond.) (Talk about the brick, wood, or of whatever the building is made.) (Read the scripture.) The 'in whom' the scripture refers to is Jesus. The building may be made from a variety of materials but it is Jesus who is the builder of the people in the church. He is the reason we have a church. He is the reason we worship; the reason we come together to study the Bible. He is the real foundation of the church.

PRAYER : Thank you, Jesus for our church and thank you for being with us today. Amen.

18
Camping With The Lord

OBJECT : Small objects used for camping.

SCRIPTURE : " Since the Lord your God walks in the midst of your camp to deliver and to defeat your enemies before you, therefore your camp must be holy." Deut. 23 : 4 NASB

LESSON : (Show the objects.) Let the children tell you what the objects are and how they are used.

(Ask). Who has gone camping? Did you enjoy it? How would you like to camp all the time?

(Read the scripture). (Say) The Lord was talking to the people of Israel. During this time in history the people of Israel moved from place to place. They did not live in houses like we do today. The Lord promised to lie in the "camp" and to watch over them, but their camp must be holy. Today, God will live in our home, in our town, but we must make our homes and towns places that are pleasing to Him.

PRAYER : Thank you dear God for promising to be with us, for promising to live in our home, and for watching over us. Amen.

19
Children And Sponges

OBJECTS : a kitchen sponge and colored water

SCRIPTURE : "Hear my son, your father's instruction, and do not forsake your mother's teaching." Proverbs 1 : 8 NASB

LESSON : [Show the sponge, and then show how quickly it absorbs the water and how the water affects the color of the sponge.]

[Read the scripture.] [Say.] The writer of the proverbs is simply telling you boys and girls to listen to your parents. They want what is best for you. You are probably here today because they saw that you came. Your parents will tell you many, many good things in your life; many of those will be stories about Jesus. Listen to the stories. Be like the sponge that soaks up the water until it can barely hold any more. As you listen to the teaching of your parents, you will become affected by those teachings just like the water colors the sponge. Your life will be better for following the instruction of your parents.

PRAYER : Thank you, Our Father for the teaching in the Bible. Thank you for mothers and fathers that teach their children about you. Amen.

20
Christian Giver

OBJECT : An offering envelope.

SCRIPTURE : "On the first day of every week, each one of you should set aside a sum of money in keeping with his income, saving it up, so that when I come no collection will have to be made."   1 Corn. 16 : 2 NIV

LESSON : (Show the offering envelope). (Let the children tell you what it is, what it is used for and when it is used.)

Paul, the missionary, was writing to the believers in Jesus. The believers had sent him to tell others about Jesus. He asked them to give their offering each week. When he returned from his missionary trip, they would have enough money to help him return to his mission work.

Through churches working together many missionaries are sent to tell people about Jesus. They depend upon our offerings. We need to give our money regularly to help them continue their work.

PRAYER : Our Father, Help us to be generous with our money and our lives. Amen

21
Direct Dial

OBJECT : Telephone with a dead battery

SCRIPTURE : "Be anxious for nothing, but in everything by prayer and supplication with thanksgiving let your requests be made known to God." Phil. 4 : 6 NAS

LESSON : [Show the telephone.] [Ask.} How many of you like to talk on the phone? [Ask.] Could we talk on this phone? Why not? It is not plugged in and it has a dead battery.

There is one call that we can make that requires no phone. We can talk to God anytime, anyplace. We speak to him and he hears our prayers. We can be thankful for the telephone. Through it we can keep in touch with family and friends. Through prayer we can keep in touch with the best friend of all, our Lord.

PRAYER : Thank you, God for hearing us when we speak to you. In Jesus name. Amen.

22
Do Good In Secret

OBJECT : a megaphone or microphone

SCRIPTURE : "But when you give alms, do not let your left hand know what your right hand is doing." Matthew 6 : 3 NASB

LESSON : Show the megaphone or the microphone.][Say.] These magnify or increase the sound of your voice. When I hear loud talking it bothers me. It bothers me even more if that person is bragging about all the good things they do. It seems they only do good things so they can tell about them. None of us like that attitude.

The Bible tells us "when you give alms (alms are good deeds) not to let anyone know about it." God knows the good things we do and that is what matters.

PRAYER : Thank you our Father, for helping us to get joy in doing for others. Help us to get double joy when just you and we know about it. Amen.

23
Don't Wear Out

OBJECT : Rusty nail

SCRIPTURE : " Go to the ant, O sluggard (lazy man); observe her ways and be wise." Proverbs 6 : 6

LESSON : (Show the rusty nail.) (Ask.) What makes the nail rusty? Yes, it has just been lying around in the weather and hasn't been used.
   (Read the scripture.)
   (Say) The little ant is very busy. No time for laziness. The Bible says we should be like the ant. We need to keep our bodies and our minds busy doing good things. Let's be like the ant and not the rusty nail. We will be useful to God and others.

PRAYER : Thank you O Lord, for chores and good things that keep us busy. Amen

24
Ears To Hear

OBJECT : Picture of an ear.

SCRIPTURE : "The ear of the wise seeks knowledge." Proverbs 18 : 15 b NASB

LESSON : (Show the picture of the ear.) (Ask) What do we do with our ears? Do we see with them? No, we hear with our ears. What do we hear? (Read the scripture) The Bible says that if we are to be wise our ears will seek knowledge. That means that you will listen to your Sunday school teacher, to your mother and daddy, to your pastor, to your schoolteacher. Listen to those persons. They want to help you.

In order to listen with our ears we need to be quiet. Listen more and learn more.

PRAYER : Our Father, help us to know when to listen. Help us to listen to teaching and to learn about you. In Jesus name Amen.

25
Equal But Different

OBJECT : A box of chalk - all colors and sizes.

SCRIPTURE : "For God so loved the World that he gave his only begotten son that whoever believes on him should not perishb but have eternal life. "John 3 : 16. NAS

LESSON : (Read the scripture.) This may be one of the first verses of the Bible that you will learn. It tells us that Jesus came to be the Savior of all people. He came to be your Savior. He loves all of us in the world the same.

Let's look at the box of chalk. Each piece is different, but it is still chalk. We are all different but we are still God's children and he loves each of us.

PRAYER : Thank you O Lord, for loving each of us. Amen

26
Everlasting Love

OBJECTS : a piece of decaying wood, tarnished jewelry, torn clothing

SCRIPTURE : "Give thanks to the God of gods, for His loving kindness is everlasting." Psalm 136 : 2 NSAB

LESSON : {Show the piece of wood, the tarnished jewelry, torn clothing.} [Ask.] What does each of these have in common? They are wearing out. They are no longer new. The jewelry is not shiny; these items are almost beyond use. [Read the scripture.] The Bible tells us that God's loving kindness lasts forever and forever. Today many objects wear out quickly; many things are used once and discarded. It is a good feeling to know that love, God's love, never runs out. We can count on it always being there for us. All we need to do is turn to him; he is there. That is a wonderful fact.

PRAYER : Thank you Dear God for your everlasting love. Amen.

27
Fears

THOUGHT : We can trust Jesus to take care of our fears.

SCRIPTURE : " In peace I will both lie down and sleep : For thou alone, O Lord, dost make me dwell in safety." Psalm 4 : 8 NASB

LESSON : (Ask)? Are you afraid in the dark? Do you become afraid of strange sounds at night? Are there others things that you are afraid of : high places, dogs, snakes? Most of us have something that we are afraid of. (Let the children share some of their fears).

(Say). The Bible has something to say about fear. (Read the scripture). We are told in this verse that the Lord helps us to dwell in safety. He will calm our thoughts and help us not to be afraid.

When you are afraid, think about this Bible verse. Think about Jesus.

PRAYER : Help us, O Lord, not to be afraid of unknown sounds and things that we see only in our minds. In Jesus Name Amen

28
Get Your Rest

OBJECT : alarm clock

SCRIPTURE : " Or do you not know that your body is the temple of the Holy Spirit?" 1 Cor. 6 : 19 NASB

LESSON : [Show the alarm clock. Let the alarm sound.][Ask.] Does anyone have trouble getting up when the alarm goes off or when one of your parents awaken you in the mornings? Do you have to be dragged out of bed or do you bounce out of bed ready for the day? The alarm tells us when to get up but our bodies may be tired and not want to wake up.

[Read the scripture.] The Bible tells us that our bodies are very special. Therefore we should take care of them. We need to get rest and eat the right foods.

The next time that you don't want to go to bed and to get your rest, remember that your body is special. Take care of it.

PRAYER : Thank you for making our bodies so special. Thank you for your spirit that helps us make good decisions concerning rest. Amen.

29
God Sees The Heart

OBJECT : A catalogue of children's clothes.

SCRIPTURE : "I the Lord search the heart." JER. 17 : 10 NASB

LESSON : Show the catalogue of children's clothes. (Ask) How many of you like to get new clothes? Why? (Let the children respond.) Do you feel good when you are all dressed up in new clothes? New clothes are okay. We like to look our best.

(Read the Scripture.) Where does God say he looks? He looks at our heart. That is another way of saying that God sees our actions, our thoughts, what we really are. How we look may be important to others; how we act is important to God.

PRAYER : Our Father, we thank you that you love us regardless of our clothes, and that you see us as we are. In Jesus name, Amen

30
God's Protection

OBJECT : an umbrella

SCRIPTURE : "For he will give His angels charge concerning you, to guard you in all your ways."Psalm 91 : 11 NASB

LESSON : {Show the umbrella.} [Ask.] When do you use the umbrella? Do you like to watch the rain? We use the umbrella to keep from getting wet. It doesn't stop us from being in the rain but it protects us from the rain. It keeps us dry.

{Read the scripture}. God promises us that he has given his angels charge over us to guard and protect us. We may still be in the midst of problems but God will be with us. Like the umbrella keeps us from getting wet, God will be there in the situation to help us.

PRAYER : Thank you Father for the great protection. Thank you for watching over us. Amen.

31
Good Work

OBJECT : A well-worn work glove.

SCRIPTURE : "And what so ever you do in word or deed, do all in the name of the Lord Jesus, giving thanks through Him to God the Father." Colossians 3 : 17 NSAB

LESSON : [Show the glove.] (Say) This glove reminds me of hard work. It is well worn and dirty showing that it has been used. Not all work is done with gloves on. We have many, many different kinds of jobs. The jobs are many but the Bible tells us how all jobs are to be done. Let's listen to the Bible.
  (Read the Scripture).
  Whatever we do that is good should be done in the name of Jesus. Our jobs should be pleasing to Him. Whatever you do, do it as though you were doing it for Jesus.

PRAYER : Our Father help each of us to remember that you are in charge of our lives. May the things we do please you. Amen.

32
Guiding Light

OBJECT : Picture of streetlights.

SCRIPTURE : "Let your light so shine before men in such a way, that they may see your good works, and glorify your Father which is in heaven." Matthew 5 : 16 NAS

LESSON : (Show the picture of the streetlights.) (Ask) Do you have streetlights or a dawn to dusk light outside your house? (Let the children respond.) (Say) The lights keep us from falling as we walk in the dark. The light shows us the way.

(Read the verse) (Say) Jesus teaches us how to live. When we live the way the Bible teaches, we become a light for other people. They can watch how we live and not fall into bad habits. In a way, we become a guiding light for others.

PRAYER : Our Father, thank you for being our light and help us to light the way for others. Amen.

33
Information Please!

OBJECTS : A sign that says "Information!", the Bible

SCRIPTURE : "Make me know thy ways, O Lord, teach me thy paths. " Psalm 25 : 4 NASB

LESSON : (Show the sign.) (Ask) Have you seen an information sign in a hospital or other public places? What is the purpose of these signs? These signs help you find your way while you are in the building. Without help from the information desk you could get lost.

(Show the Bible.) This book has in it information that we need every day. It tells us how to treat others, how to treat ourselves and most importantly, it tells us how to find God.

When you see an information sign, remember another very important source of information, the Bible.

PRAYER : Thank you God for the Bible that helps us in all we do. Amen.

34
Jesus Calms The Storm

OBJECT : picture of clouds, of a storm, or of lots of rain

SCRIPTURE : Luke 8 : 22- 25 NASB

LESSON : {Show the picture.] [Ask.] Do you like storms? Are you a little afraid if you are caught in a storm? We often talk about Jesus' power to heal, his power to help people be better, and his power to forgive. Jesus also had, and has power over nature. [Tell the story.] Jesus and his disciples were on the lake in a sailboat. As they sailed, Jesus fell asleep. There came a storm. The boat filled with water, and they were in danger. The disciples awoke Jesus and said, "Master, Master, we are sinking."

Then Jesus arose and spoke to the wind and the water. There was a calm. He said to his disciples, "Where is your faith?"

Let us remember not only the mighty power of Jesus, but also the wonderful way that he cares for us.

PRAYER : Thank you Dear Jesus for your strength and your tender loving care. Amen.

35
Jesus Wept

OBJECT : A branch of a weeping willow tree or picture of a weeping willow tree.

SCRIPTURE : "Jesus wept." John 11 : 35 NASB

LESSON : Show the picture of the weeping willow tree or the branch. Let the children tell you what it is. [Say.] The branches of the weeping will sway long and low almost like its head is bowed in sadness.

Have you had a time when you felt very sad? Maybe it was a time when someone very close to you died. [Read the Scripture.] Jesus was sad. His friend had died; the Bible says that he cried or wept. It is okay to show that we are sad. It is okay to cry. Jesus understands how we feel because he has felt the same way. We can talk to him about our feelings. Let us pray.

PRAYER : Thank you Jesus for understanding how we feel. Thank you for hearing us when we pray. Amen.

36
Joyful Noises

OBJECT : Jingle bells tied with a ribbon (One for each child)

SCRIPTURE : "Make a joyful noise unto the Lord" Psalm 100 KJB

LESSON : [Say the verse. Have the children say it with you a couple of times.] [Ask,] "What are some joyful noises that we make in church? We sing. We listen to the piano, to the organ, to the scripture. We think of joyful noises as those made with a happy voice or music that comes because the heart is happy. When we come into God's house, we can come with happy hearts because Jesus is our friend and because He loves us. When we sing, let's sing with happy hearts. [Give each child a set of bells] here is something that makes noise. Let's all shake them together. Let that be our joyful noise today. Take them with you to remind you make joyful noises to God.

Prayer : Thank you our Father for hearing our prayers, for encouraging us to make happy sounds that honor you. Amen.

37
Kind Words

OBJECT : a picture of children talking

SCRIPTURE : "Keep your tongue from evil and your lips from speaking deceit." Psalm 34 : 13 NASB

LESSON : {Show the picture.} [Say.] These boys and girls look like they are having a good time. Let's imagine what they are saying. Maybe they received good grades at school and they are happy. Maybe they are going to take a trip with their Sunday School class. They must be talking about happy things because they look happy. [Read the scripture.] The Bible tells us to speak of good things. We are not to speak of evil things. We are not to tell bad things about people. Let us remember to keep our words kind. Let's make our words please Jesus.

PRAYER : Thank you dear God for telling how we should talk. Help us to keep our words kind. Amen.

38
Live In Harmony

THOUGHT : " We are to be people who love peace."

SCRIPTURE : " If possible, so far as it depends on you, be at peace with all men." Romans 12 : 18 NASB

LESSON : Have you heard these words, "He is a peace loving person"? Or maybe you have heard this; "He is a trouble maker."

Your parents may have said to you, "Don't stir up trouble." " Don't pick at your brother or sister."

Fighting and fussing are not peaceful. These stir up trouble. People get their feelings hurt and they begin not to like one another when they fuss a lot.

The Bible teaches us to try to live in peace. We are to be caring people and not fighting people. {Read the scripture.}

PRAYER : Thank you, Our Father, for teaching us to live in harmony with others. In Jesus name, Amen.

39
Love - Not Revenge

OBJECT : boxing gloves, picture of people fighting

SCRIPTURE : "See that no one repays another with evil for evil, but always seek after that which is good for another and for all men." I Thess. 5 : 15 NASB

LESSON : {Show the boxing gloves or the picture.] [Ask.] Do any of you ever fight? [Allow the children to respond.] When do you fight? I suppose most of us get angry from time to time. We may even fight when another does something bad to us. The teacher may call your Mom or Dad and say, "Jimmy and Bobby were fighting. Jimmy took Bobby's pencil and Bobby hit him." (Read the scripture.)

What does the Bible say about fighting? It says to seek the good for another person. We are not supposed to be bad to another just because they were bad to us. If we all did this, there would constantly be fights and problems. When we return a bad deed with a good one, we are helping bring about peace. It makes our world a better place to live.

PRAYER : Thank you Lord for giving us the strength to do good when others treat us badly. In Jesus name. Amen.

40
Love One Another

OBJECTS : Tiny sticker hearts or hearts cut out of construction paper with "love" written on them. Tape the back so they will stick on each child.

SCRIPTURE : " Walk in love, as Christ also hath loved us." Eph : 5 : 2 a.NASB

LESSON : (Read the scripture) (Say) In this scripture the writer, Paul, tells us to walk in love. In other words, we are to make love a part of our daily life. It's easy to love Mom, Dad or our family. If we "walk" in love, we will love everyone. Everyone many include the classmate that you don't like or your worst teacher. God helps us to love everyone. When we love others, we will feel good inside and we will help others feel good.

(Say) I'm giving you a little heart to remind you to love others. You can take an extra heart and place it on someone to show your love.

PRAYER : Thank you dear Jesus for loving us and showing us how to love others. Amen.

41
Measured To Overflowing

<u>**OBJECT**</u> : an old-fashioned peck measure, a bushel basket, etc.

<u>**SCRIPTURE**</u> : "Give and it will be given to you, good measure, pressed down, shaken together, running over, they will pour into your lap. For by your standard of measure it will be measured to you in return." Luke 6 : 38 NASB

<u>**LESSON**</u> : [Show the object. Let the children identify it, if they can.] Fill the measure with something dry such as seed or meal. Fill it lightly, and then shake it down. Explain how the material settles. Now read the scripture. [Say.] Jesus spoke these words. He tells us how to give. In other words, don't be stingy; don't be selfish. If you borrow from a friend, pay it all back plus some. As you are generous, you create a generous spirit in your life. Remember these words from Jesus as you share with others. God will bless you with kind and generous hearts.

<u>**PRAYER**</u> : Father, thank you for these words that Jesus spoke. Help us to be kind and generous in our actions toward other people. Amen.

42
Milky Way

OBJECT : Small candy bars (Milky Way) for each child.

SCRIPTURE : "In the beginning God created the heavens and the earth." Genesis 1 : 1 NASB

LESSON : [Read the scripture.] The Bible tells that God created the world, not just the earth that we live on, but the entire universe. It is planned so perfectly - for the good of God's children. We are responsible for taking care of his creation. We take care of it, but God did the creating.

On a dark night, out away from the city lights- it seems there are a billion stars twinkling. One part of the universe that God created is called the Milky Way. It stretches across the horizon and its bright appearance is due to many, many stars so distant and so blended that they can be distinguished only by an extremely powerful telescope. Yet, God made this part of the universe, also.

Let's pray; let's thank God for his greatness and his love for us.

PRAYER : Father, thank you for creating us, for the universe and for holding it all in place. Amen.

[Give each child a candy bar to eat later.]

43
Not To Brag

THOUGHT : Most of us do not like to hear another tell how much they know, or talk about how good they are.

SCRIPTURE : "Let us not become boastful, challenging one another, envying one another." Galatians 5 : 26 NASB

LESSON : {Read the scripture} [Ask.] How do you feel when another is always bragging about how good they are, about their good grades, how they are the best in football? Not many of us like to be around people who brag. The scripture gives many guidelines to live by. We all need to read the Bible and find instruction there. (Read the scripture verse) This verse tells us not to brag or boast, not to want what another has. We are to care about each other, to love each other. If you have a tendency to boast or brag, then you need to change. Think about how the other person feels. Let others talk and listen to them.

PRAYER : Thank you O Lord for teaching us in the Bible how we should live and how to get along with each other. In Jesus name. Amen.

44
One God

OBJECT : Picture of idols or things that people worship.

SCRIPTURE : "One God and Father of all who is over all and through all and in all."   Ephesians 4 : 6 NASB

LESSON : (Show the pictures.) (Say) People of other religions claim these to be their God.

(Then say.) There is but one God. He speaks to us through the Bible. We cannot see him, but we can feel his presence in our heart and minds.

He answers our prayers. We can depend upon him. The Bible tells us that there is only one God; we are to worship him only.

PRAYER : Thank you Dear God for being greater than we can understand; for being so simple that we can trust you. Amen.

45
Our Daily Bread

OBJECT : a slice or a small loaf of bread

SCRIPTURE : "Give us this day our daily bread." Matthew 6 : 11 NASB

LESSON : [Show the slice or loaf of bread.] [Ask.] How many of you eat bread each day?

Bread is one of our basic foods. It is one that we say is necessary for life. Bread is referred to as "the staff of life."

[Read the scripture.] This scripture is from the "Lord's prayer".

Jesus asked for daily bread. Often we want a lot of things that we don't need, things that clutter our lives and our rooms.

Jesus just says, "Give us this day our daily bread." Just give us what we need for today. This is the way we must trust God. He will supply what we need each day and meet our needs as we trust in him.

PRAYER : Thank you Jesus for teaching us how to pray. Help us to be content with what we have and to use it to help others. Amen.

46
Overtired

OBJECT : shows a picture of an individual carrying a large load on his back.

SCRIPTURE : "Come to me, all who are weary and heavy laden, and I will give you rest. Matthew 11 : 28 NASB

LESSON : {Show the picture.] [Ask.] Do you think that this man is tired? What could he do to ease his burden? He could stop and rest but he would still have to pick up his load and carry it. What else could he do? He could leave part of it but he needs all that is in the load. What could he do? He could ask another person to help him.

[Read the scripture.] Do you have a problem that `weighs' you down or really upsets you? You have a friend who is ready to help. Jesus tells us in this scripture to let him share our problems. We can always talk to him.

PRAYER : Thank you Dear Jesus for your love, for your help in sharing our problems. Amen.

47
Practice, Practice

OBJECT : A ball to bounce, or small cheap balls to give each child

SCRIPTURE : "My son keep my words and treasure my commandments within you." Proverbs 7 : 1 NASB

LESSON : [Ask.] How many of you like to play ball? Can you catch a ball? Bounce it? All these take practice. [One pastor did a little juggling act that the children loved.] [Read the scripture.] [Say.] In the Bible God gives us rules to live by. "Do not lie;" "do not steal"; "honor you mother and your father;" "love God."

There are others. We must practice the rules so that we can remember them. We must follow the Bible's teachings daily; not just occasionally. Just as practice makes a good ball player, practicing God's teachings makes us a better person.

PRAYER : Thank you God for helping us to be better people. Help us to practice your rules for living. In Jesus name. Amen.

48
Pray Out Loud

OBJECT : Picture of a child praying.

SCRIPTURE : "Let us therefore come boldly into the throne of grace, that we may obtain mercy, and find grace to help in time of need." HEB. 4 : 16 KJV

LESSON : (Read the Scripture. Show the picture of the child praying).

Once a little boy, very ill, lay on the couch. His mother sat at his side rubbing his back and comforting him.

He said, "Mommy, will you pray for me?"

His mother replied, "Of course I will," and she prayed silently for her son.

In a few minutes he asked, "Mommy, did you pray?"

"Yes, I did," she said.

"Please, pray out loud Mommy."His mother than prayed aloud so he could hear. Soon he felt better and went to sleep.

Sometimes, we need to let others know that we are praying for them. We need to let others know that we care for them.

PRAYER : Our father, help us to pray for others and to let them know that we are praying. Comfort us in our hard times and help us to comfort others.

Amen.

49
Priority Mail

(Christmas)

OBJECT : A stamped package that says, "Priority mail".

SCRIPTURE : " For unto us a child is born, unto us a son is given; and the government shall be upon his shoulder; and his name shall he called wonderful counselor, the mighty God, the everlasting Father, the Prince of Peace." Isa. 9 : 6 KJV

LESSON : (Show the package). (Say) We are nearing Christmas. Many of us will be mailing packages. I sometimes use "Priority mail" because I know then when the package will arrive. (Ask) Why do we celebrate Christmas? Jesus was born. (Read the scripture). These words were written many hundred years before Jesus was born, telling the people to expect his birth. When God knew the time was right, he made the preparations and Jesus came just at the right time. He was a "priority" package sent right on time by God. That's why we celebrate Christmas.

PRAYER : Thank you God for that gift of Jesus who came to be our friend and our Savior. Help us to celebrate him this Christmas. Amen.

50
Recipe For Happiness

OBJECT : A cookbook.

A recipe card for each child with the scripture, Ephesians 4 : 32 written on it. "Be kind to one another."

SCRIPTURE : Ephesians 4 : 32 NASB

LESSON : (Show the cookbook.) (Let the children tell you what it is.) (Ask) Who uses this book the most in your house? (Let them tell you some of their favorite foods.)

(Say) I am going to give you a recipe that you can keep. It is not an easy recipe but it brings good results.

(Read the verse.) "Be ye kind to one another." It tells us how to treat each other. It didn't come out of the cookbook. It came out of the Bible.

Keep this little card to remind you of God's recipe for happiness, kindness.

PRAYER : Thank you Lord for teaching us to be kind to each other. Amen.

51
Remote Control

OBJECT : Remote control

SCRIPTURE : "The Lord has heard my supplication, the Lord receives my prayer." Psalm 6 : 9 NASB

LESSON : [Ask.] Who can tell me what this is? Yes, it is a remote control to the television. By pushing the button, I can control the channel selection and turn the television on and off. I do not understand how it works but I don't have to understand how it works; I just need to know how to push the button.

We may not understand how praying to God works or how he hears. We don't have to understand we just need to pray. It will work.

[Read the scripture.]

PRAYER : Thank you Lord for hearing our prayer and for loving us. Amen.

52
Repairman

0BJECTS; Needle, thread and piece of mended cloth

SCRIPTURE : "He heals the broken - hearted and binds up their wounds. "Psalm 147 : 3 NASB

LESSON : [Let the children tell you how the needle and thread are used.] [Say.] We use them to repair our clothes or torn places in fabric. [Show the piece of material that has been mended.] [Then say.] There is another kind of repair work, the kind that Jesus does. When we are upset or lonely, we can talk to Jesus and he can help or mend and repair our hurt feelings. He makes us feel better as we read the Bible and as we talk to Jesus in prayer. {Read the scripture.} He does heal or mend broken hearts.

PRAYER : Thank you Jesus for helping us feel better when we are sad or lonely. Thank you for caring for us. Amen.

53
Reserved Dates

OBJECT : a calendar with the Sundays marked in a special way.

SCRIPTURE : "Worship the Lord with reverence." Psalm 2 : 11 NASB

LESSON : {Show the calendar.} [Say.] Why do you think the days are marked in red? That's right. Those days are Sunday. What is so special about Sunday? We may do a lot of things on Sunday. We may go to Grandma's house for lunch; play outside; read. The Bible tells us to "worship the Lord with reverence" and Christians have chosen to worship Him on Sunday. God set aside a day for us to rest and to worship. The rest helps our bodies; the worship helps our soul. God didn't set this rule to punish us, but to help us. He knows that both our bodies and our spirits need rest. Our worship helps us become closer to God and to be more like him.

Remember to mark your calendar each week and worship God.

PRAYER : Thank you dear God for a day of rest and worship. Amen.

54
Resist Bad Things

OBJECT : An overhead lampshade that has dead bugs in it.

SCRIPTURE : "Resist the devil, and he will flee from you." James 4 : 7 KJV

LESSON : Show the lamp and the dead bugs. (Say) The lamp was bright. Its warmth seemed good to the bugs. What seemed good really wasn't. Because they stayed too close to the lamp they became too hot and died.

There will be things in your life that may seem okay, things that others are doing but these will harm you. Older boys and girls are tempted with alcohol and other drugs. These may seem okay at first but like the warm lamp they tend to hold you and eventually destroy you. Decide now that you will have nothing to do with these harmful substances. God tells us to resist anything that harms our bodies. By not beginning bad habits, we will not be caught by them.

PRAYER : Dear Lord, I pray that you will protect these little ones from bad habits and wrongs that might harm them. Amen.

55
Rich In Good Works

OBJECT : A stack of play money.

SCRIPTURE : "Instruct them to do good, to be rich in good works, to be generous and ready to share." 1 Tim 6 : 18 NASB

LESSON : (Ask) What does it mean to be rich? Have a lot of money? Own a lot of property? Drive a fancy car? Maybe it means different things to different people.[Let the children share what `being rich' means.]
   (Read the scripture)
   The scripture says to be rich in good works. We are to be busy doing good for others. That is to be our goal in life, to help others, to be generous and ready to share.
   We all like folks who share easily, not many of us like folks who are stingy. God tells us to be generous.

PRAYER : Thank you, our Lord, for helping us to be generous. Amen.

56
Rock Or Sand

OBJECTS : A rock and a jar of sand.

SCRIPTURE : Matthew 7 : 24-27

LESSON : [Show the rock; show the jar that is about half full of sand. Tilt the jar to show how the sand moves around.] (Ask) Imagine that this rock was as large as the room and that the sand was a beach, which place would you build your house? The sand would wash away and the house would fall.

In the Bible Jesus compares the man who built on the sand to the person who hears the Bible and does not follow its teaching. They are foolish.

Listen as I read the story. [Read the scripture in an easy to understand version of the Bible or from a Bible storybook.]

(Say) Let's be like the wise man that built his house on the rock as we obey the Bible.

PRAYER : Our Father we thank you for giving us instructions in the Bible on how to live. Amen.

57
Seeing Eyes

OBJECTS : set of 'button' eyes bought in a sewing or craft shop

SCRIPTURE : "Son of man, you live in the midst of the rebellious house, who have eyes to see but do not see, ears to hear but do not hear, for they are a rebellious house." Ezekiel 12 : 2 NASB

LESSON : Give each child a set of eyes that you have glued to a piece of wood, paper, shells, etc. [Ask] Can these eyes see? [Let the children tell you why they think the eyes cannot see.] [Read the scripture.] [Say.] There are some big words in this reading. The meaning is that some people do not see the right way because they do not want to see the right things. You have eyes, however you may not see because you were not looking. Choose to look at the good things, good television shows and good books that mom and dad help you select. Do you know this little song?
[You and the children can sing the little song together.]
Oh! Be careful little eyes what you see.
Oh! Be careful little eyes what you see.
There's a savior up above watching over you with love.
Oh be careful little eyes what you see."

PRAYER : Thank you dear Lord for eyes to see the beautiful things that you have made. Help us to use our eyes for good things. Amen.

58
Smallness - Greatness

OBJECT : Some very, very tiny flowers that bloom in spring and early summer. Usually you can find these in the grass.

SCRIPTURE : " Rejoice in the Lord always; again I will say, rejoice!" Phil. : 4 : 4 NASB

LESSON : (Show the tiny flowers.) (Say)

Most of the time these tiny little flowers go unnoticed. Even though they are very pretty, they are just too small to be seen. Yet, if you look for them you will see just how lovely they are.

Throughout your life there will be joys that will go unnoticed unless you search for them. Begin now, looking for those small blessing from God. Thank him for each little thing that makes you happy. If your friend shares a candy bar, thank him and God! If your parents take you to get an ice cream cone, thank them and God! Rejoice in the joys that come whether they are large or small and you will be a happier person. You will form a lifelong habit of being grateful.

PRAYER : Thank you dear God for all the joys you bring to life. Amen

59
Something For Nothing

THOUGHT : Simple Simon met a Pieman
Going to the fair.
Said Simple Simon to the Pieman.
"Let me taste your ware."
Said the Pieman to Simple Simon.
"Show me first your penny."
Said Simple Simon to the Pieman
"Indeed, I have not any."
Mother Goose

SCRIPTURE : "Providing for honest things, not only in the sight of the Lord, but also in the sight of men." 2 Cor.8 : 21. KJV

LESSON : (Read the nursery rhyme). (Ask) What was Simple Simon's problem? He wanted a piece of pie but he had no money. It seemed he was going to taste now and pay later. Isn't that the way we are sometimes? We want things we do not have money for. Like the pie, often it is something we do not have to have. Simple Simon was asking for that for which he could not pay. The Bible teaches us to be honest with others. (Read scripture). You are never too young to learn to be honest. Don't take that which is not yours.

PRAYER : Our Father, Help us to live our lives honestly before you and before our friends. We pray in Jesus name. Amen.

60
Stain Removal

OBJECTS : Several stained objects and bottles or boxes of stain remover.

SCRIPTURE : "Come now, and let us reason together," says the Lord, "though your sins be as scarlet, they will be as white as snow." Isaiah 1 : 18 NASB

LESSON : [Show the different objects. Point out the stains. Show the stain remover. Explain how the stain remover helps - by making the object look like new again.]

[Read the scripture.]

[Say.] In this verse, sin is referred to as a stain. Just as stain ruins our clothes, sin messes up our lives. If we lie, steal, say unkind words about others, we are staining our lives. There is one who takes away the stains in our lives. As we pray to God and ask his forgiveness, we become fresh and renewed. Our lives become as clean as the snow is white.

PRAYER : Our Father, thank you for making our lives clean, thank you for forgiveness of our sins. Amen.

61
Stretching The Truth

OBJECT : a good sock and one with badly worn elastic

SCRIPTURE : "You shall not bear false witness against your neighbor."
Exodus 20 : 16 NASB

LESSON : [Show the two socks. Explain that one is new and the other
has been stretched all out of shape.]
　　[Read the scripture.]
　　[Say.] Truth is a lot like the new elastic in the new sock. It is fresh,
unchanged, and ready for the task. However, truth can be repeated and
changed until it becomes like the ruined sock. It only faintly resembles
what it started out to be. It has become a lie. It is ruined and cannot
be made back like it once was. Words spoken cannot be taken back.
Think before you speak. Be sure that what you say is true. Do not
'bear false witness' or in plainer words, "Do not lie."

PRAYER : Help us our Father to be careful what we say about others.
Help us to keep our words kind, loving and true. Amen.

62
Supplies For A Happy Day

OBJECT : Book bag or pencil box with school supplies

SCRIPTURE : " The desire of a man is his kindness." Proverbs 19 : 22 KJV

LESSON : Open the box or book bag. (Ask). What supplies do you need for school or kindergarten? A ruler, marker, pencil, and paper are some of the things that you will need. Let's think of other things that we can put into our bag that will make a happy day for you and for others.

Let's put in a "thank you" for the teacher and classmates. Then let's add a "smile for the principal". What about a "please" for the helpers in the lunchroom and a "big hug" for mother when you come home. All these are kind acts that make others feel good. " The desire of a man (or child) is his kindness". The Bible teaches us to be kind to others.

PRAYER : Dear Lord, I pray that you will be with these children. Help them to grow up knowing how special it is to practice kindness. Amen.

63
Take Care Of The Earth

OBJECT : A large piece of coal - or if you are in an area where children are unfamiliar with coal, give each child a small piece wrapped in a plastic bag. Be sure to tell them not to open it until they have permission.

SCRIPTURE : Then God said, "Let us make man in our image according to our likeness; and let them rule over the fish of the sea and over the birds of the sky and over the cattle and over all the earth, and over every creeping thing that creeps on the earth." Genesis 1 : 26 NASB

LESSON : (Read the scripture). [Show the block of coal. If they know, let the children tell what the coal is and what it is used for.]
(Say). Coal is one of our natural resources. It is found deep under the ground and has to be dug out either by hand or by machine. Coal is used for many things including heating our homes. Like our other natural resources the coal can be used up. According to the scripture, God made man to be in charge of the world. We are to be careful with the things for which God has made us responsible. Ways that you can help are by saving water, keeping doors closed so you won't lose heat in the house, by not littering. In these ways and many others we take care of what God has given us.

PRAYER : Thank you, Dear God for giving us this place to live. Help us to take better care of the world. Amen.

64
Teach Me Thy Way

OBJECTS : An empty bag, Bible, picture of a church, picture of a family

SCRIPTURE : " Make me know Thy ways, O Lord Teach me Thy paths." Psalm 25 : 4 NASB

LESSON : (Show the children the empty bag.) (Read the scripture.) (Say.) Like the Psalmist, let's think of some ways we are taught to follow God's path. Let's pretend that the empty bag is our lives. Think what we can use to fill it with good things.

(Let the children make suggestions.) (Show a Bible.) This is God's written word. It teaches us how to live. (Show a picture of a church). This is God's house. We learn about Him in his house. (Show a picture of a family.) Our family can help us learn about God. Let's put these items in our bag. Now let's thank God for these.

PRAYER : Thank you God for our Bible, for our church and our family. Amen.

65
Tell The Truth

OBJECT : A can of shaving cream.

SCRIPTURE : " Ye shall not steal, neither deal falsely, neither lie to one another." Lev. 19 : 11 KJV

LESSON : Show the shaving cream. (Say) Who wants to push the button? Let each child push the button. (Catch the cream on a paper plate).

(Say) Who will volunteer to put the shaving cream back in the can? It is impossible to put the cream back in the can.

(Read the scripture). When a lie is told, it is like the shaving cream. It can't be taken back. It gets told and retold. It does much damage. Be very careful what you tell others. Be sure that it is true and that it will not harm another person.

PRAYER : Our father, help us to be careful what we say. Help us to remember to speak the truth. Amen.

66
The Best Artist

OBJECT : Paint brushes, a piece of canvas, or artist paper.

SCRIPTURE : "The heavens are telling of the glory of God; and their expanse is declaring the work of his hands." Psalm 19 : 2 NASB

LESSON : {Show the artist paintbrush and canvas.} {Allow the children time to tell you how these are used. [Ask if they like to paint.]

[Read the scripture.] [Say.] When you look at a beautiful sunset or billowy clouds in the sky, do you think about God? Remember that God is the creator of the world. Did you notice how beautifully the colors all match? The greens, yellows, blues, reds etc. God put the world together in a wonderful way. We often are concerned about matching the colors of the clothes we wear. Let's remember that God is the best artist of all. He matched up the colors of the world. Let's remember to thank him for this beautiful place we live.

PRAYER : Thank you dear God for this beautiful world; for all the color and beauty that surrounds us. Amen.

67
The Best Law

OBJECT : The Bible, a gavel or law book.

SCRIPTURE : " Teach me Thy way, O Lord; I will walk in Thy truth."

Psalm 86 : 11 NASB

LESSON : (Show the gavel or law book.)

(Say) When you are very young, your parents begin to teach you the laws or our country and state. Cross the street when the sign says WALK. Don't litter.[Name some others or let the children name some.] The law helps us to live together. It helps us to live safely. It sets boundaries of right and wrong for us to follow.

Likewise the Bible sets boundaries for us. It is the law of life for Christians. When we follow the Bible's teaching we will live a happier life.

(Read the Scripture)

PRAYER : Dear God, thank you for your law that teaches us how to live. Thank you also for the policemen that protect us and for the laws that we live by in our country. In Jesus Name. Amen

68
The Burning Bush

This little story would be good for an outside meeting with children. It requires a little more showmanship than the others do but I found that the children enjoyed it a lot. *A word of caution to be very careful.*   Una.

OBJECT : A large western style handkerchief, 70% rubbing alcohol, water, metal tongs with <u>wood</u> handles and matches. (Mix equal parts of the alcohol and water).

SCRIPTURE : Exodus 3

LESSON : Tell the story to the children about the burning bush in words that the children can understand.

(Say) Now we are going to do a little project that will help you remember about the day God called to Moses from the burning bush.

Soak the handkerchief well with the alcohol-water mixture. (*Stand away from the children*). Hold the handkerchief at one corner with the metal tongs. Have an adult set it on fire at the bottom. It will blaze completely. Just as the blaze dies down, give a quick jerk to put out all the fire that might be left. Let the children fell the cool handkerchief and see that it isn't burned at all.

Caution Stand a little ways from the children; use metal tongs; practice once*.

PRAYER : Thank you Lord for calling Moses, for his great leadership. Thank you for still calling people today to serve you. Amen.

69
The Greatest Healer

OBJECT : a doctor bag or medical supplies

SCRIPTURE : " And seizing him by the right hand, he raised him up, and immediately his feet and his ankles were strengthened." Acts 3 : 7 NASB

LESSON : {Show the articles.] [Say.] We are thankful for doctors and for medical personnel. When we are sick, we are even more thankful because they help us to feel better.

Jesus was not a medical doctor but he and his disciples often healed people.

There was a lame man who had *never* walked. The only way that he could make a living was by begging. He stopped the disciples, Peter and John, and asked for money. Peter told him the he had no money but he commanded him "in the name of Jesus" to be made well. The Bible says that the man began to walk and leap and praise God. He had been made well. God still gives the power through the means of medicine to heal. Still there are times when he heals impossible cases just like the case of the lame man. Let us thank him for his compassion and love.

PRAYER : Thank you Dear Jesus for using your power to make our lives complete. Amen.

70
Thirst Quincher

OBJECT : Water in a glass with ice and straw.

SCRIPTURE : "As the deer pants for the water brooks, so my soul pants for thee, O God. My soul thirsts for God, for the living Lord." Psalm 42 : 1 NASB

LESSON : Show the glass of water. Stir the ice cubes.

[Ask.] On a hot summer day, how many of you like a big glass of ice water? Just thinking about it makes me thirsty. Imagine hiking in the mountains. You have drunk all your water and you come to a cold, clear spring of water. You are so thirsty that your tongue is dry. Doesn't the water look great!

[Read the scripture.]

The deer gets thirsty and looks for the water hole. God tells us that we are to look for him with the same kind of sincerity as a deer looks for the water when he is thirsty.

PRAYER : Thank you Lord for being there when we look for you and for responding to our call. In Jesus name. Amen.

71
Treasures In Heaven

OBJECT : computer diskette

SCRIPTURE : "But store up for yourselves treasures in heaven, where neither moth nor rust destroy and where thieves do not break in and steal." Matthew 6 : 20 NASB

LESSON : [Show the diskette. Ask.] Who can tell me what this is? [Allow for response.][Say.] This is a computer disk. Pages and pages of information can be stored on this little disk. You could put the little disk in the computer, push a few buttons and there is the information. Before the disk can be helpful the information has to be stored on it.

Jesus tells us to "store up treasures". The treasures that he is speaking about are not money but knowledge, wisdom, kindness and good things. One way we learn these is from reading the Bible, from Bible stories. Then, when we need God's help the source is in our minds; we only have to recall it. First, it must be put there. Listen to the Bible and store good things in your mind.

PRAYER : Thank you Lord for our minds where we can store good thoughts and ideas that come from you. Amen.

72
Unmeasured Love

OBJECTS : measuring spoons and measuring cups.

SCRIPTURE : "See how great a love the Father has bestowed upon us that we should be called children of God."1 John 3 : 1 NASB

LESSON : {Show the measuring spoons and cups.} [Ask.] How many of you have watched your mother or grandmother make cookies? They may measure a cup of shortening, 2 cups of flour, 1/2 cup sugar, etc. Each ingredient calls for a different measure.

[Read the scripture.] [Say.] When God gives to us, he gives to each of us a measure of his love. He doesn't give one cup to one of you, 2 cups to another. He gives freely and equally to all of us. It is up to us to accept that love. Remember his measure is the same for all of us.

PRAYER : Thank you Father for the great love that reaches out to each of us. Amen.

73
Vessels For God

OBJECT : A Kitchen pot

SCRIPTURE : "He will be a vessel for honor, sanctified, useful to the Master, prepared for every good work. " 2 Tim. 2 : 21

DEVOTION : (Show the Kettle)
(Say) This kettle is used in the kitchen for cooking. In order to be used the kettle needs to be clean. It cannot have holes in it. It must be taken care of.

(Read the Scripture) (Say) This verse of the Bible says to be used by God; we must be faithful to Him. He will take care of us and he will help us to be useful to Him and to His work.

PRAYEER : Thank you dear Lord for helping us to be useful in your kingdom. Help us to be your vessels. Amen.

74
What Is A Friend

OBJECT : A sticker or a piece of paper with the scripture verse on it; "A friend loveth at all times." Proverbs 17 : 17 NASB

SCRIPTURE : " A friend loveth at all times." Proverbs 17 : 17 NASB

LESSON : [Show the verse; Talk to the children about friends. [Ask]. Who is your best friend? Do you enjoy being with your friend? Why do you like to be with your friend? Does the friend like you? [Say] One of the best things about friends is that they love us. We can count on them. They like us back! The Bible tells us that "A friend loveth at all times." They don't just love us when we have some candy or are going to do something special. A friend loves us all the time. Let us bow and thank God for friends.

PRAYER : Lord, thank you for sending us friends. Thank you for being our friend. In Jesus Name. Amen.

75
What Is A Martyr?

OBJECT : Write the word MARTYR on a piece of poster board.

SCRIPTURE : "Acts 6 : 8 – 15 NASB

LESSON : {Show the word.] [Ask.] Who can tell me what this word is? Do you know what it means? A martyr is one who is willing to give everything - even their life for a cause that they are committed to - for something that they really believe in!

In the Bible we can read about Stephen who was a Christian martyr. He was one of the men that Jesus' disciples chose to help them. The Bible tells us that he was full of faith. There were those that disliked him so much that they told lies about him. He remained true to his belief in Jesus even when they had a trial to test him. Finally, the people stoned him to death. He never betrayed Jesus or those principles that Jesus taught. He died saying, "Lord Jesus receive my spirit". Thus, he was a Christian martyr. There have been missionaries and others who have been killed rather than deny Jesus. We may never be asked to die for Jesus, but we can give Him our life as we love and serve Him.

PRAYER : Thank you Dear Jesus for your power and your love that makes life worth living. Amen.

76
What Is A Soul?

OBJECT : a shoe or the sole of a shoe

SCRIPTURE : "He restores my soul; he guides me in the paths of righteousness.' Psalm 23 : 3 NASB

LESSON : [Show the shoe. Let the children identify the parts of the shoe : the tongue, strings, and soles. Talk about the sole.]

The shoe sole is not seen however it is very important. It gives support to your feet. It keeps your feet from getting wet and dirty.

[Read the scripture.] The psalmist was talking about another kind of soul. Our soul is the most important part of us. It is the part of us that relates to God and to other persons. In reality it is who we are. Once in a while our soul may be troubled or sad. What does the scripture say God does? He restores my soul. Just as the shoemaker may repair the sole on your shoe, God restores our souls. We can praise him for that.

PRAYER : Thank you Lord, for restoring us; for making us like new again. Amen.

77
What Is Your Name?

OBJECT : a nameplate, identification badge, blank nametags [the stick on kind] that children can put their name on.

SCRIPTURE : "For a child will be born unto us, a son will be given unto us, and the government will rest on His shoulders, and his name shall be called Wonderful Counselor, Mighty God, Eternal Father, Prince of Peace." Isaiah : 9 : 6 NASB

LESSON : [Let each child tell you his or her name. Say] before you were born, your parents may have carefully selected your name. That name is very special because it identifies you.

Another special name to us is "Jesus". God chose his name long before Jesus was born. That name identifies who Jesus was to be and is. The prophet used these words to identify Jesus many hundred years before he was born. He would be a wonderful counselor, a mighty God, the prince of peace, and our eternal father.

Jesus is all of these and much more! Let us thank him for who he is.

PRAYER : Thank you Jesus for all that you are and for coming to the world to show us how to live. We pray in Jesus name. Amen.

78
What's In The Wrapper

OBJECT : Wrapped pieces of chewing gum or candy. Have some candy wrapped in gum paper and gum wrapped in candy paper. (Have one for each child).

SCRIPTURE : "Study to show thyself approved unto God." II Tim.2 : 15 KJV

LESSON : (Show the piece of chewing gum or wrapped piece of candy.)

(Say) The wrapper tells us what is inside. If I put the gum wrapper on a piece of candy and give it to you, what do you expect to see when you opened the wrapper?

(Read the scripture.) We are to study God's word and live as it says. We may tell others that we love Jesus but unless our actions show that we belong to Him, others will be confused. They will know that we belong to Jesus by the way we live. What is seen on the outside tells who we are.

PRAYER : Our father, help us to study the Bible, to live by its teaching and to show love to others. Amen.

79
Who Is The Judge?

OBJECT : A courtroom gavel

SCRIPTURE : " Do not judge lest you be judged." Matthew 7 : 1 NASB

LESSON : [Show the gavel; allow the children to examine it and tell you what it is.][Ask.] Have any of you been in a courtroom?] [Say.] The judge uses the gavel to call the court to order. The judge makes decisions when people are brought before him. After he hears the facts, he carefully decides if the individual before him is guilty or innocent.

Sometimes we like to act like a judge; we may talk about others, saying things that are not true. The Bible tells us not to act like judges. We do not know all the facts and it is not our place to judge or to condemn others. We have earthly judges, however God is the only one who knows all about each of us. He is the final judge in our lives.

PRAYER : Lord, forgive us for not always being kind in our thoughts and speaking of other persons. Help us not to judge others. In Jesus name we pray. Amen.

80
Wise With Money

OBJECT : A piggy bank

SCRIPTURE : " He that gathereth in summer is a wise son, but he that sleepeth in harvest is a son that causeth shame." Proverbs 10 : 5 KJV

LESSON : [Show the piggy bank.] (Say) You may have a bank at home where you save your money. (Read the scripture). The Bible teaches us many things. One of those is to live a balanced life. It teaches us to share our money, to return some to the Lord's work, not to keep it all for ourselves, not to be wasteful, to save something for later. The scripture refers to gathering in the summer when food is plentiful and saving some for the time when there is nothing. Remember the Bible teaches that if we are wise, we will save; we will plan ahead and always give thanks to God for what we have.

SCRIPTURE : Dear Lord, thank you for food and other ways you provide for us. Help us to use what we have in a way to please you. Amen.

81
X-Ray Vision

OBJECT : an exposed x-ray of the lung or some obvious part of the body.(A hospital radiology laboratory should be happy to save a discarded one.]

SCRIPTURE : "Search me, O God, and know my heart; try me and know my anxious thoughts; and see if there be any hurtful way in me, and lead me in the everlasting way." Psalm 139 : 23 NASB

LESSON : {Show the x-ray to the children. Point out the body part.] [Say] Doctors use the x-ray to look inside our bodies. They can find broken bones; find out if we have pneumonia or other things. How many of you have had an x-ray? We can be thankful for this procedure because it helps the doctor to treat us and make us well.

[Read the scripture.] God has a way of seeing our needs and our problems. He knows what we are thinking. We might say he has `X-Ray' vision. Let us be thankful that he sees and understands us.

PRAYER : Thank you Dear God for knowing all about us and for taking care of us. Amen.

82
You Are Important

OBJECT : Picture of Jesus and the children.

SCRIPTURE : " And he took them (the children) in His arms and began blessing them."   Mark 10 : 16 NASB

LESSON : (Show the picture of Jesus and the children). [Let the children tell you who is in the picture.] (Ask) Do you ever wonder what Jesus is like? We don't have an actual picture of Jesus but the Bible describes him. He was gentle and strong. He was a kind teacher that loved people. He loved children. In several places in the Bible Jesus talks lovingly about children.

If you ever wonder if children are important, remember that Jesus loved the children. You are important. (Read the verse).

PRAYER : Thank you Jesus for loving all of us. Amen.